BY MOONLIGHT AND SPIRIT FLIGHT

BY MOONLIGHT AND SPIRIT FLIGHT

The Praxis of the Otherworldly Journey
To the Witches' Sabbath

MICHAEL HOWARD

THREE HANDS PRESS

By Moonlight and Spirit Flight

Second Three Hands Press edition, December 2019.
First published 2013 as part of the Three Hands Press
Occult Monograph series.

Cover Image: *To the Sabbat*, by Benjamin A. Vierling, 2019.

Typogrpahy and layout by Joseph Uccello.
Cover and jacket design by Joseph Uccello
and Daniel A. Schulke.

ISBN 978-1-945147-34-0 (softcover)

Manufactured in the United States of America.

THREEHANDSPRESS.COM

The first time she was involved with the Devil was when she was but a lass and was tending herds in the fields. A heaviness came over her near a hill, and presently a big headless man came to her asking whether she was asleep. She said, I am neither asleep nor awake. In his hand, he was holding a large ring of keys which he offered her, saying, If you accept these keys, all that you wish to undertake in this world will come to pass.

—TRIAL OF KAREN EDISATTER, 1620

Demons & Witches Gather at the Sabbat, J. Benlliure, from *La Ilustracion Espanola Y Americana*, November 1880.

T HE Sabbat of the Witches, as depicted in late medieval and early modern lore, is populated with a great number of denizens and fantastic ritual elements. The dead and the living flock together in a nocturnal convocation, their circle lit with lamps of burning fat and attended by demons and satyrs. Alternately horrific and erotic, the scenes of the Sabbat utilise a combination of phantasmagorical features to convey an atmosphere of dark ecstasy which has given rise, in part, to the modern conception of the witch. These tableaus are an amalgam of Christian heresies and the iconography of pagan myth, also at times incorporating local folklore.

One important and recurring feature of the Witches' Sabbath is the element of flight: the airborne retinue of witches, their animal mounts and spirits travelling in procession through the night sky to a distant ritual gathering in some remote location. Though the flight of the witches is commonly relegated to the fantastical elements of legend, its basis lies, in part, in actual magical practice, most of which has been obscured by the historical record.

In an essay entitled 'Provenance, Dream and Magistry', Andrew D. Chumbley (1967–2004), an Essex cunning man, traditional witch and sorcerer, gave a description of the Sabbatic Craft as he had inherited it from his initiators. He defined the term as describing "an ongoing tradition of sorcerous wisdom, an initiatory path proceeding from both immediate vision and historical succession." He goes on to say that "An important dimension of magical and folk religiosity was the oneiric or dream realm." He relates this to "the oneiric location of witch- meetings, faerie convocations and the nocturnal flight of the Wild Hunt". This in turn relates to the fact that the Witches' Sabbath is

> *the astral or dream convocation of magical ritualist's souls, animal selves and a vast array of spirits, faeries and Otherworldly beings. It is considered that the location of the Sabbath is at the crossroads of waking, sleeping and dreaming, that is the state of True Dreaming—the realm in which the Lady Moon, the nocturnal sun, illumines a world beyond the reach of the uninitiated.*[1]

Typically, the constructs of the Witches' Sabbath are examined by historians and folklorists from a micro-historical and mytho-folkloric perspective. What sets Chumbley and his traditional witchcraft group and magical order the *Cultus Sabbati* apart is that a group of modern practitioners of folk magic,

---

1 Chumbley, A. *Opuscula Magica* Volume 2, pp. 97–100.

emerging from the milieu of 19th century English and Welsh cunning folk, inherited an historical set of practices and some of these featured the mythos of the Witches' Sabbath. This seems to have arisen as a conscious and mystical adoption of a witchcraft folklore usually held to be malignant, or the identification of Sabbatic elements in long-established charming and spellcraft practices.[2]

Chumbley regarded the mythos of the Witches' Sabbath, as it was derived from medieval and early modern European accounts, as the defining feature of the Sabbatic Craft as he had been taught it, and of the tradition he subsequently founded. In fact, the Cultus Sabbati is a group of traditions as it embraces and consists of several inherited and reified streams of the Old Craft historically originating from Essex, Wales, Shropshire and Cornwall. Chumbley rejected any idea that the use of this mythos and imagery was in any way dwelling on the past. On the contrary he saw it as "a spirit-taught reification of the Sabbath's potent oneiric reality in an ongoing tradition of magical practice."[3]

Within the precincts of the Cultus Sabbati and the Sabbatic Craft in general, the complex, ancient and eldritch imagery of the Witches' Sabbath is regarded as an atemporal reality of ritual praxis. Chumbley said that when perceived through ritual practice, dreaming and mediumship, "the myriad motifs of the Sabbath yield new wisdom and serve as wholly apposite ciphers for the teaching of onei-

2 Ibid.
3 Ibid.

ric flight [and] atavistic transformation." He went on in his essay to affirm that the symbolism of the Sabbath has been used to encode the accumulated and still developing teachings within the Cultus. This is through the magical technique known as 'ritual as dreamt', where symbols and images received in the oneiric state are then translated into rituals in the waking state, and it forms the basis and context of the tradition. This magical art of True Dreaming is produced by "active discourse between initiates and our spirit patrons..." and it manifests in "...text, ritual, performance, song, tapestry, craftsmanship or image."

FACING PAGE: Division of the Self into distinct spirit-fractions as induced by Sabbatic Conciousness. Andrew D. Chumbley, "Erotocrasis: The Arch of Drewary O'er the Sigillick Tree of Earthen Albion", from *Azoëtia: A Grimoire of the Sabbatic Craft* (1992, 2002).

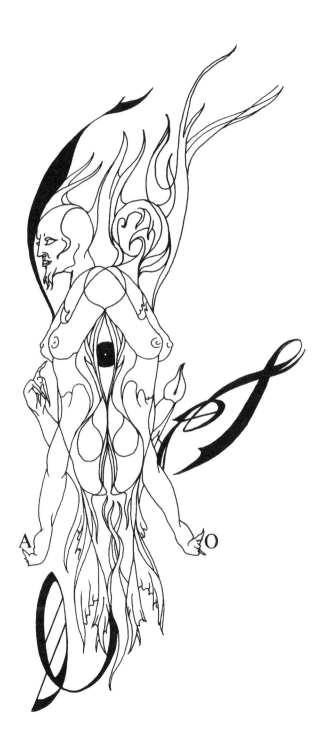

It is specifically the spirit-flight to the Witches' Sabbath and the art of True Dreaming, and its praxis within the traditional form of witchcraft known as the Sabbatic Craft, that I wish to examine in this essay. To do so, we must first look at the subject of dreams and dreaming as experienced in a mundane context. Psychologists, in their usual rational way, have divided dreams into various categories such as traumatic dreams, nightmares, anxiety dreams, oedipal dreams, convenience dreams, orgiastic (sexual) dreams, alienation dreams, recurrent dreams and imperative dreams.[4] All these dream types are based on psychological or physical manifestations of the dreamer's consciousness and are deeply rooted in a materialistic view of dreaming. In contrast, the ancients regarded the dream realm as "the world of the gods, spirits, or ancestors."[5]

In Ancient Greece it was believed that the Gods and other spirits could enter a bedroom through the keyhole while its occupant was asleep. It was also believed that the dreamer could leave his or her body and travel to the other side of the world or even visit the spiritual realm. In esoteric terms, we would refer to this as the projection of the astral body or spirit body and astral or spirit travel. Modern researchers into the paranormal refer to it as 'out-of-body experiences' or (OOBES) and the CIA, who have experimented with such psychic techniques, call it 'remote viewing'. This process of spirit travel was a two-way journey as the spirits could also

---

4 Rycroft, C. *The Innocence of Dreams*, pp. 98–129.
5 Watkins, M. *Walking Dreams*, p. 15.

enter this world through the dreams of the sleeper. It was not only "a bridge from one world to another, but...a plane of co-existence of the two worlds." As a result of this intercourse, the dreamer was able to "obtain gifts of wisdom and self-knowledge from the divine benefactors."[6]

The temples of Ancient Egypt and classical Greece and Rome had special priests known as 'oneirocrits'. Their role was to supervise dream incubation rituals and interpret the dreams of worshippers. In the more than three hundred temples dedicated to dream incubation in the classical world visitors would spend the night sleeping within these temples' precincts. It was believed that the patron god of the temple would then appear to them in a dream and relate information. The morning after, the priest would interpret the symbols and images the sleeper had received from the spirit source. The 20th century Swiss psychologist Carl Jung interpreted symbols seen in dreams as archetypal images arising from the collective unconsciousness of the human race.[7] Jung had an interest in astrology, alchemy and Gnosticism and he was fully aware of the true nature of dreams and their importance as a means of communication with other realms of existence.

There is a belief in cultures worldwide that sorcerers have the magical ability to fly through the air. Specifically, it is claimed in popular European folk belief that the witch used this method of transportation to travel to their meetings known as the

6 Ibid.
7 Jung, C. *Memories, Dreams, Reflections*. p. 325.

Witches' Sabbath. Even the Protestant reformer Martin Luther believed that the spirit of witches flew abroad while their physical bodies remained at home. One of the earliest references to night-travelling witches is found in a 10th century manuscript *Canon Episcopi*. This describes how witches "ride on certain beasts with Diana, goddess of the pagans, and a great multitude of women...over great distances in the silence of the deep night." One of the earliest illustrations of witches in flight, depicted with either animal heads or wearing animal masks and riding astride forked sticks or stangs, dates from the late 15th century. However, in the 13th century Stephen of Bourbon had written that the 'good women' (witches) who attended Dame Habondia (one of the medieval names for the witch goddess) rode on sticks to the Sabbath.

By the time the European witch trials began in earnest, it was generally accepted by the Inquisition and civilian witch-hunters that witches could physically fly through the air on sticks, besoms, animals, hurdles and even plants to their meetings. Obviously, it is not physically possible for a human being to fly so we must look for an alternative explanation for this widely held belief. Nigel Aldcroft Jackson has explained it in terms of 'spirit flight', which was a state of ecstasy entered into by the witch during which he or she experiences "a flight both through states of perception and also through various Otherworlds".[8] In 1647 the philosopher and poet Henry More wrote:

---

8 Personal communication, 1991.

And 'tis an art well known to Wizards old
And wily Hags, who for fear and slave
Of the coarse halter, do themselves withhold
From bodily assisting their right game
Wherefore their carcasses do home retain
But with their souls at these bad feasts they are
And see their friends and call them by their name
And dance about the Goat...
And kiss the Devil's breech, and taste his deadly cheer.[9]

One of the artificial aids allegedly used by the historical witches to facilitate their journey to the Sabbath as described above by Henry More was the so-called *unguentum sabbati*, flying ointment or 'lifting balm'. In the 17th century a nun called Sister Madeliene de Demandolx from the convent at Aix-en-Provence in southern France told the Inquisitors who questioned her that "the sorcerers by the power of a certain ointment which they use are carried in the air by devils..." to the Sabbath.[10]

This so-called flying ointment consisted of a mixture of naturally narcotic and hallucinogenic plants and herbs. These psychoactive botanicals included wolfbane or aconite, belladonna (deadly nightshade), poplar leaves, smallage (wild celery), sweet flag, cinquefoil, parsley, henbane, mandrake, hemlock, and opium. The ingredients were mixed into a paste using, according to the witch-hunters, the fat of unbaptised babies, bat's blood and soot. In reality something like goose fat or lard would have

---

9 Cited in *Poems*, Manchester University Press, UK edition 1931.
10 Quoted in Russell Hope Robbins, *Encyclopedia of Witchcraft and Demonology*, p. 419.

been used as the base material for the ointment. Bat's blood and soot were both ingredients added for purposes of sympathetic magic, as bats can see in the dark and soot conceals white skin during the night.

The botanical elements in the flying ointment include a number of psychoactive plants known for both their occult symbolism and narcotic properties. Aconite is sacred to the Greek goddess of the underworld, witchcraft and sorcery, Hecate. It is said to have originated from the saliva of the three-headed dog Cerebus who guards the gates to Hades. Cinquefoil was a plant used by medieval magicians to increase the powers of communication and induce dreams. Parsley was used in scrying and was sacred to the Greek underworld goddess Persephone. Henbane was regarded in folklore as a plant of death and magically was used to evoke spirits. Mandrake is a renowned magical plant surrounded by legends and is said to increase psychic perception. Hemlock is another underworld plant with associations with death. In the lore of occult correspondences, it is ruled by Saturn, and in the medieval grimoire *Key of Solomon* hemlock juice is recommended to consecrate the athame or black-handled ritual knife.

On a medical level the plants used in the witches' flying ointment have significant physical effects on the human body. For instance, aconite depresses the cardiovascular system and in high doses it can produce irregular heartbeats and paralyzes the nervous system. Atropine, which is the principal ingredient of belladonna, causes extreme excitability, followed by delirium and finally unconsciousness. The irregular action of the heartbeat, possibly combined with oxygen restriction to the brain, would cause a person falling asleep to experience the sensation of falling through space. Combining this with atropine might well produce a feeling of flying through the air.[11]

The actual use of a flying ointment by historical witches is attested to by evidence from the witch trials and by contemporary accounts from reliable eye-witnesses. One early instance where a flying

The witches of the Blocksberg, Germany "engaged in their appalling, blasphemous and lascivious practices, assisted by their diabolical friends". 17th century engraving.

11 See Kuklin, A. *How Do Witches Fly?* pp. 25–32 and 81–92, and Hansen, H. *The Witch's Garden*, p. 101.

ointment featured in a witch trial was the case of
Dame Alice Kyteler in 14th century Ireland. When her
husband died in mysterious circumstances, the finger of suspicion was pointed at this aristocratic
Norman-Irish lady. Eventually she was charged with
various serious crimes such as denying Christianity,
practising sorcery, making sacrifices to demons, per-
forming death magic and sexually consorting with
an incubus spirit. Dame Kyteler's house was searched
and 'a pype of ointment wherewith she greased a
staff, upon which she ambled and galloped through
thick and thin, when and in what name she listed'
was discovered.[12]

In 1560 the writer Giambattisa Porta claimed
that a witch had promised to bring him some information from a distant town without going there.
She shut herself in her room while Porta watched
through the keyhole as she got undressed, smeared
her naked body with an ointment and fell into a
deep trance. Porta entered the room and attempted
to wake her up from the trance, even to the extent
of beating her so badly that she was black and blue
with bruises all over her skin. When the woman
finally came out of her trance, she described her
travels over mountains and seas and provided Porta
with the information he wanted.

At the trial of the Somerset witches in 1664, Eliza-
beth Style said that when she travelled to the Sabbath
she anointed her wrists with a greenish ointment
given to her by the 'Man in Black'. She then recited
a charm saying "Thout tout, about throughout and

12 Byrne, P. *Witchcraft in Ireland*, p. 25.

about" and flew through the air to the witches' meeting place. When she wanted to return home, she said RENTUM TORMENTUM. Styles added: "Sometimes they attended the Sabbath in their body and sometimes without, yet they knew each other." This reflected the view of the French witch-hunter Nicholas Remy who stated:

> *Witches do often really and in fact travel to their nocturnal synagogues; and sometimes again such journeys are but an empty imagination begotten of dreams.*

In some cases of 'flying witches' it was believed that the practitioner shapeshifted into the form of an animal by administering the *unguenti sabbati*. In the Lorraine area in 1599 a suspected witch said she met the Devil who undressed her and rubbed her naked body with "a certain grease he had." This had the effect of transforming both her and her companions into cats. In this form they could easily enter the house of a person they wanted to poison by going through the window slats of his or her bedchamber. The judges at the trial were sceptical of this confession as they did not believe that the Devil had the power to transform a human into a small animal. In response the accused insisted that what she had told them was the truth and it had happened.[13]

The author of the 15th century grimoire *The Book of the Sacred Magic of Abramelin the Mage* reported a

---

13 Briggs, R. 'Dangerous Spirits: Shapeshifting, Apparitions, and Fantasy in Lorraine Witchcraft Trials' in *Werewolves, Witches and Wandering Spirits*, pp. 11–12.

young witch in Austria who demonstrated the use of the flying ointment to its author Abraham the Jew. She gave him a salve and when he rubbed it into the palms of his hands he immediately fell into a deep sleep and experienced the physical sensation of flying. On another occasion the witch used the ointment on herself and claimed to have travelled over a long distance and observed the activities of a friend of the magician.

In 1545 Pope Paul III's personal physician tested a sample of a flying ointment that had been confiscated by the Inquisition from a witch. He found a woman volunteer and applied the unguent to her body. She fell into a deep sleep that lasted thirty- six hours and when she awoke described strange dreams. In 1555 the wife of a public hangman who was responsible for executing witches decided to test the flying ointment on herself. She anointed her body from head to foot and fell into an unconscious state. After several hours she awoke and told her bemused husband that she had been with a lover who was both younger and better than him.[14]

The Kent lawyer and sceptical writer on witchcraft, Reginald Scot, did not accept the stories that witches could fly. He challenged a witch he knew to demonstrate the magical art of flying to him and his companions. She ordered them to leave the room while she undressed and smeared her body with ointment. Apparently, Scot spied at the woman through a hole in the door and saw her fall to the floor and lose consciousness. Although the

14 Andrews, G. *Drugs and Magic*, p. 276.

Witches' Sabbat. Frontispiece of Collin de Plancy's
Dictionnaire Infernal—1818.

men banged loudly on the door, she did not stir for several hours. When she finally awoke she told Scot she had travelled to many other lands while she had been asleep.[15]

In modern times Gustav Schenk has described the unpleasant effects of taking henbane (*Hyoscyamus niger*), a toxic plant belonging to the nightshade botanical family. He reported that it caused his teeth to clench together involuntarily and feel angry for no reason. He also felt that his feet and head were lighter than the rest of his body and were breaking loose from it. Significantly, he also experienced a sensation of flying through the air over a surrealistic landscape containing strange looking plants and animals, slowly falling leaves and molten flowing rivers.[16]

Another modern experiment with the witches' salve was carried out in the early 1960s by a German university professor, Dr Erich Will Peuckert, using a recipe from Johannes Baptisa Porta's book *Magia Naturalis* (Natural Magic) written in 1568. The ointment's ingredients included thornapple, wild celery, parsley, henbane and belladonna. Instead of the fat of unbaptised babies, Dr Peuckert used ordinary lard from a grocer's shop. The professor tested the salve on himself and asked a lawyer friend to be both a witness and co-participant in the experiment. The friend was unaware of the purpose of the experiment or the alleged effects of the ointment.

15 *Discoverie of Witchcraft*, p. 165.
16 Andrews, p. 276.

Early in the evening both men applied the ointment liberally to their foreheads and armpits and within a short time they had fallen into a deep sleep. This state lasted for nearly 24 hours and when they awoke, they had sore throats, severe headaches and extremely dry mouths. Without first talking to each other, the two men independently wrote down their experience while they had been unconscious. When these were compared they described similar sensations of flying through the air, landing on a mountain—one of the typical European locations for the Witches' Sabbath—dancing wildly with naked women and bizarre rituals involving the worship of a Devil-like creature.[17]

Dr Peuckert explained away his experiences while under the influence of the flying ointment by suggesting that the narcotic botanical elements in it had created chemical reactions in his brain, causing hallucinatory dreams. He assumed the medieval witches could not distinguish between the experiences they had in the trance-like state induced by the salve and everyday reality. However, this does not explain the similar experiences reported by the witches and those non-witches, like the professor and his colleague, who have tested the flying ointment.

There is some anecdotal evidence that certain psychoactive plants can act on the pineal gland. This physical organ in the body occultists claim is the site of the so-called 'Third Eye' that can trigger astral projection and other psychic experiences. At a

17 Peuckert, W. "Hexensalben" in *Medizinischer Monatsspiegel 8.*

talk given at the Quest Conference in Bristol several
years ago attended by the writer, Dr Serena Roney-
Dougal described this process and how she had experienced it among South American shamans. She
claimed that shamanic practitioners in the Amazon
rain forest can project their spirit bodies to 'remote
view' cities in Brazil they have never seen. Dr Roney-
Dougal also linked their knowledge of psychotropic
plants and their effects on the Third Eye with the
use of flying ointments in European witchcraft.[18]

From 1994 to 1998 Daniel A. Schulke, the present Magister of the Cultus Sabbati, participated in
a closed magical group that experimented with the
unguenti sabbati. During their investigations into the
subject, a large number of recipes for the traditional
flying ointment were found in historical sources and
tested for their efficiency. In practice these were also
combined with various magical techniques such as
prayer, chanting, dancing and scourging. The principal ingredients used included belladonna, opium, hemlock, henbane, poplar and smallage with
the addition of mandrake, thornapple, mugwort
and tobacco. In the rituals, extracts of mugwort
and wormwood were found to be successful in fa-
cilitating a trance state. Participants also reported
physical effects such as the attainment of a form of
ecstasy and a disembodied sensation that in some
ways reflected the alleged experiences of a nocturnal flight to the Witches' Sabbath. However, many
of the experiences, though inducing states of trans-

18 Ronay-Dougal, S. *Where Science and Magic Meet*, p. 87.

formed consciousness, did not conform to historical descriptions of the Sabbath.[19]

In addition to the use of narcotic and psychedelic herbs in the *unguentum sabbati*, there is also an historical tradition in witchcraft of the ingestion of psychoactive plants, especially in a mycological form. The two principal examples are the so- called 'magic mushroom' *Psilocybe semilanceata* and *Amanita muscaria* or the fly agaric toadstool with its distinctive white-spotted red cap. It has been claimed that fly agaric was used by the traditional witches' coven in the New Forest into which Gerald Gardner, the founder of modern Wicca, was initiated into in 1939.[20] Gardner visited the poet Robert Graves, author of *The White Goddess*, at his home in Majorca in 1961. Interestingly one major topic of conversation was the experiments carried out by Gardner's own coven at Brickett Wood in Hertfordshire with 'magic mushrooms'.

In an essay entitled 'The Golden Chain and the Lonely Road', Andrew D. Chumbley discussed the various types of initiation into the Old Craft. One form is what he calls entheogenic initiation or the Witches' Supper and it involves the sacramental ingestion of natural psychotropic agents in a magical context. Among those Chumbley lists are belladonna berries, hemp (hashish), Syrian rue, black hellebore and fly agaric or 'Crow's Bread'.[21] In practice, such entheogens are used in an elixir or potion taken by

19 Schulke, D. *Veneficium: Magic, Witchcraft and the Poison Path*, pp. 146, 157 and 163.
20 King, F. *Ritual Magic in England*, p. 141.
21 A folk-name for magical intoxicants, of Essex derivation.

the candidate for initiation after he or she has been mentally prepared by their sponsor into the Craft. After drinking the potion, the candidate is left alone in a remote place such as a wood, a rural churchyard or a prehistoric burial mound. Afterwards they are questioned about their experiences during the nocturnal vigil. Chumbley also mentions in his essay the use of the *unguentum sabbati* or Devil's Salve by practitioners of traditional witchcraft to "leave the flesh" and ride astrally with the Wild Hunt.[22]

The sorcery of colonial North America, especially amongst Native Americans of the Southwestern United States, possessed a number of notable Sabbatic features, including nocturnal flight of the spirit. Also present in these regions was a potent local pharmacopeia. Of prime importance were the visionary cactus peyote (*Lophophora williamsii*), and the hallucinogenic thornapple, a relative of the European witch-herbs henbane, belladonna, and mandrake. Although specific references of an ointment made from these plants for spirit-flight are scant, unguents of 'Devil's Weed' or datura—drunk to induce initiatic visions and also locate lost objects—were made for medicinal purposes, including anæsthesia. When the Spanish encountered the native sorcery of such tribes as the Zuñi, the Pueblo and the Navajo, it was frequently described as witchcraft, seen as it was through the filter of European witch-belief.[23] Practices of certain magical societies such as the Navajo Skinwalkers, who went forth by

22 Chumbley, A. *Opuscula Magica* Volume 1, pp. 106 and 108.
23 Simmons, M. *Witchcraft in the Southwest: Spanish and Indian Supernaturalism on the Rio Grande*, pp. 152–155.

night to stalk power, enemies, or otherwise inno-
cent victims, bear a striking resemblance to other
nocturnal spirit-wanderers of European origin, such
as the *mazzerei* of Corsica.[24]

The flying ointment and other drugs are artificial
aids that assisted the witch to leave his or her body
in spirit form and travel 'out and about'. However,
there was also a strong folk belief that the witch
could send her 'fetch' or spirit double, without the
use of any ointment, and it could actually be seen
by those and it detached itself from its physical host
either during a trance-like state, in sleep or just before death. It was described as a physical replica of
the human body and in this form, or in the guise of
a small animal such as a weasel, rabbit or mouse, it
could either physically visit people or appear in their
dreams. In one Norse saga a man called Thormod
receives a visit in a dream from an old friend who
tells him: "You are dreaming but what will appear
to you will seem as though it had appeared to you
in the waking state."[25]

The idea that the witch's fetch could also appear in animal form gave rise to the legend of the
werewolf and the many stories of witches turning
into hares. It is also possibly linked with tales of
vampires visiting their victims at night, as in Central
and Eastern European folk tradition witches and the
Undead were often synonymous. If the fetch was in-
jured in any way, then there would be a corresponding wound on the human body of its sender. There

24 Teller, J. and Blackwater, N. *The Navaho Skinwalker, Witchcraft and
Related Phenomena.*
25 Lecouteux, C. *Witches, Werewolves and Fairies*, pp. 29–32.

are many folk stories of hunters shooting hares, and a local woman suspected of being a witch is later found with either a corresponding wound or dead.

Belief in the spirit double and the notion that it could leave the body was not confined to pagan beliefs. In the 6th century CE, Gregory of Tours told the story of the bishop of Albi who was believed to have died after suffering a high fever. Several monks kept an all-night vigil by his body as was the custom and were surprised in the morning when it began to move. When the bishop came to from his death-like state, he remembered having visions. The Christian monk and historian the Venerable Bede wrote in the 8th century about an Irish priest who "died one night and came back to life the next morning" and then reported what had happened to him.[26]

In 1489 the role of the spirit-double or fetch in witchcraft was mentioned by Ulrich Molitor in a story about St Germain. One night the saint was staying in the cottage of a humble peasant. He noticed that before retiring, his host had prepared a second meal and laid it on the table, even though it seemed he was not expecting any more guests. Later St Germain found that the meal had been consumed by 'evil spirits' and these appeared in the form of the man's neighbours. Molitor used this tale to demonstrate that "at the precise moment a man is in one place, nevertheless he is able to appear in spirit in another..."[27]

---

26 Ibid.
27 Robbins, R. *Encyclopedia of Witchcraft and Demonology*, p. 513.

In fact, in the original account of the saint's life, published in the 5th century, Germain asks the peasant who is preparing the second meal for and he replies: "The good ladies who come by night" (witches). When the spirits or demons appear, St Germain wakes up his host and orders him to identify who they are. The peasant says they are his neighbours, whereupon the saint commands the demonic doubles to stay where they are and not move. A person is then dispatched to each of the neighbour's houses and reports back that their physical bodies are asleep in their beds. Obviously these 'evil spirits' are not demons at all, but the spirit doubles of local people who are witches.

In the 13th century a French Inquisitor called Etienne de Bourbon reported the case of a woman who believed her child was being attacked in the night by a blood-sucking witch. She decided to watch over her son and saw her neighbour, a small old woman, enter the house through a closed door and riding a wolf. As the old woman approached the cradle, the mother struck her in the face with a hot iron and she left emitting a loud cry. When the woman called on her neighbour the next morning accompanied by the bailiffs and several witnesses she was still in a heavy sleep. They could clearly see she had a burnt cheek, so she was awoken and arrested for witchcraft.[28]

Writing in the 16th century, the witch-hunter Jean Bodin said that when he was in Nantes in 1546 he heard about a group of magicians who could send

28 Lecouteux, C. *Witches, Werewolves and Fairies*, p. 78.

out their spirits from their bodies. In the presence of many witnesses they said they were going to report what was happening in a radius of seven leagues (twenty-one miles). They fell into a trance-like state in which they remained for three hours. When they awoke, they told the assembly what they had seen in Nantes and the surrounding area. This included places they had never visited, people and their activities. When this account was checked with those mentioned it was found to be true and accurate.[29]

The main use of the spirit double was to travel to the Witches' Sabbath. It is difficult to know when the belief in an organised witches' meeting originated, although early medieval accounts of the alleged activities of Christian heretics mentioned them attending 'synagogues' that are similar in nature. The Italian historian Dr Carlo Ginzburg has speculated that the Witches' Sabbath was first formulated in print by a Dominican monk called Johannes Nider in his *Formicarius* in 1437. It was based on witch trials Nider had been informed about by an Inquisitor at Evian and a judge from Berne. According to Nider, a sect of anti-Christian 'devil worshippers' had been identified sixty years before in this area. Dr Ginzburg says that these practitioners of the witch cult appeared in the Western Alps in the middle of the 14th century, about fifty years before the date usually accepted by scholars.[30]

He further claims that the emergence of popular ideas and beliefs about the Witches' Sabbath

29 Ibid., p. 87.
30 Ginzburg, C. 'Deciphering the Witches' Sabbath' in *Early Modern European Witchcraft*, p. 121.

may have been influenced by the Roman Catholic Church's previous persecution of lepers, Jews, Muslims and Christian heretics. In this historical model, heretical crimes such as apostasy of the Christian faith and the desecration of Christian symbols may have attributed to its medieval legend as witchcraft was demonized. He states:

> *Decades of inquisitional activity in the Western Alps completed the convergence between heretics and followers of the witches' sect: worship of the Devil in animal form, sexual orgies and infanticides [all allegedly aspects of Christian heresy] became invariant components of the stereotype of the Witches' Sabbath.*[31]

An example of the witch practices that were present in the Alpine region is provided by the story of a horse wrangler and herdsman called Chonrad Stoeckhlin in the 16th century in Bavaria. While working in the woods cutting down a tree, Stoeckhlin claimed to have seen the ghost of his best friend who told him to repent his sins or he would become a wandering revenant like him. The herdsman followed the spirit's advice and as a result made further contacts with the Otherworld that included a vision of an angel and experiencing travelling out of his body. He also seems to have acquired healing powers and became well known in the district as a healer treating both humans and animals.

31 Ginzburg, *Ecstasies: Deciphering the Witches' Sabbath*, p. 80.

Stoeckhlin claimed that he would fall into a trance and as he lay motionless his spirit would leave his body and travel abroad. He was not alone these excursions, as he joined up with groups of other

'Le Ronde du Sabbat'. Lithograph of Louis Boulanger, 1826.

men and women he knew as the 'phantoms of the night', who had also vacated their bodies and were in spirit form, and the shades of the dead. They often gathered together in remote meadows and danced to music that placed them under a spell. These revels went on until cockcrow and the sun rose and then they returned to their physical bodies.

Chonrad Stoeckhlin also seems to have acted as an unofficial witch-finder as in 1586 he made accusations of witchcraft against a local woman called Anne Erizensberegin. The charge was based solely on information the herdsman had received from the leader of the 'phantoms of the night'. Such was the level of superstition in the Alpine villages that the judge and jurors in Oberstdorf accepted this testimony without question. It eventually led to the woman's arrest and her subsequent death while in custody. An official investigation into the 'witches and sorcerers' of Oberstdorf then began and Stoeckhlin himself was arrested by officers acting for the bishop of Augsburg and imprisoned in Fluhenstein Castle.

Because the herdsman had talked about taking part in spirit flights and meeting the spirits of other living people and the dead at gatherings in the mountains, the prosecuting tribunal believed he was a witch. Under interrogation, Stoeckhlin admitted that he knew about witches and they also travelled through the air in spirit form, but he claimed he was never one of them. The tribunal did not believe this, and they accused him of using a witches' salve to facilitate his nocturnal wanderings. They also identified the 'phantoms of the night' as witches and sorcerers who left their bodies to attend meetings. Stoeckhlin however vehemently denied he used any artificial means to leave his body and travel in spirit.

However, the fact that Anne Erizenberegin, the woman the herdsman had accused of witchcraft, had confessed, probably as a form of revenge, that she had been taught by Stoeckhlin's mother seems to have persuaded the tribunal that he was guilty. They believed that because he was widely regarded as a 'witch doctor' and a witch-finder by local people he must have travelled with the witches at night. Several other people who had been arrested confessed under torture that they had been present at gatherings where they saw Stoeckhlin dancing with the witches. On the 23rd January 1587 the herdsman was burnt to death and he was followed by many other inhabitants of Oberstdorf as the anti-witch hysteria spread.[32]

These early accounts of witch-gatherings have also linked by Dr Ginzburg with the activities of the *benandanti* who, although they were not witches, were regarded as such by the Roman Church. In 1575 reports reached the Inquisition at Friuli in Italy of a man from the village of Isacco who cured the bewitched and 'roamed about at night with witches and goblins.' Eventually the story began to emerge of a sect of magical practitioners called the *benandanti* who battled in dreams or 'in the spirit' with malefic witches and wizards because they threatened the fertility of the crops. These 'night battles' began when the folk magicians fell into a deep sleep

---

32 Behringer, W. *Shaman of Obertsdorf.*

or trance. Their spirits then allegedly left their bodies in the form of a small animal or insect such as a mouse or a butterfly or in human form riding a dog, hare, cat or pig.

Faced with such amazing accounts, the Inquisition demonised the *benandanti* and tortured them into confessions of flight to the Witches Sabbath where they consorted with demons and worshipped the Devil. In their defence the *benandanti* claimed they were 'good witches' and were opposed to the evil type who they fought in their nocturnal spirit battles. They however confessed that they did use anointing oils or a cream smeared on their bodies to facilitate their spirit flights. One called Margherita of San Rocco, who was burnt at the stake for witchcraft in 1571, told her accusers: "The visits to the games which I have made did not take place in person, but in spirit, leaving the body at home." One of her companions said:

> *I greased myself with an ointment I had brought with me...and was transformed into a cat, left the body at home, descended the stair, and went out by the door.*[33]

The activities of the Italian *benandanti* are mirrored on the Mediterranean island of Corsica where the *mazzeri* or 'dream hunters' still exist. These are people with special gifts who travel out of their bodies at night to hunt animals such as pigs, goats, boar,

---

33 Ginzburg, C. *The Night Battles*, pp. 1–4 and 19; 'Deciphering the Witches' Sabbath' in *Early Modern European Witchcraft*, pp. 124–125.

sheep, bulls and cows. They are mostly female and hunt in packs, tearing their prey to pieces with their teeth like hounds. For this reason they have been connected to the legend of the Wild Hunt.[34] The animals they kill are said to represent real people or the spirit doubles of people in animal form and any wound inflicted on the animal is reproduced on its human representation and can lead to injury or their death.

When Dorothy Carrington asked one of her informants if he had ever actually seen the *mazzeri* kill an animal he replied; "How could I? All that takes place in dreams."[35] Carrington was told that the dream-hunters stay in their beds at night and in a trance-like state leave their bodies and travel abroad. For this reason, they are also called 'night walkers'. Witnesses have reported seeing known practitioners walking about at night on the dream hunt while their families have sworn that they were asleep in bed at home.

The stereotypical, demonised version of the Witches' Sabbath as imagined by the Inquisition largely focused on the alleged anti-Christian aspects of the gathering, although the fact that these meetings often took place on the dates of Church festivals that were previously pagan suggests they contained some ancient elements. These dates included:

34 Carrington, D. *The Dream Hunters of Corsica*, p. 58.
35 Ibid., p. 59.

FEBRUARY 1st	IMBOLG *or* CANDLEMAS
APRIL 30th	MAY EVE *or* ST WALPURGIS NIGHT
JUNE 23rd	MIDSUMMER'S EVE *or* ST JOHN'S EVE
AUGUST 1st	LUGHNASADH *or* LAMMAS
OCTOBER 31st	SAMHAIN *or* ALL HALLOW'S EVE

In fact early references to the 'good women' or witches riding at night in the company of pagan goddesses such as Diana and Holda and attending their 'games' led Dr Carlo Ginzburg to suggest that the medieval concept of the Witches' Sabbath has a pre-Christian pagan origin and was demonised by the Roman Church when the witch-hunt began.[36]

The archetypal Witches' Sabbath consisted of several distinctive elements including the assembly, homage to the presiding Devil or his human representative, the feast, dancing and finally the *orgia*. It would appear that each individual had to make their own way to the meet and, as we have seen, it was popularly believed that they flew to it on a besom or

36 Ginzburg, C. *Ecstasies: Deciphering the Witches' Sabbath*, pp. 89–121.

broomstick, a forked staff (stang), on the back of an animal such as a goat or by some bizarre form of transportation such as fennel stalks, distaffs or hurdles.

Brocken scene, artist unknown.

At first glance these methods seem unbelievable until it is realised that the hurdle, for instance, is an artificial form of the hedge. In early medieval accounts the witch was often described by the German term *hagazussa* or *haegtessa*, meaning 'hedge rider' or person who sits on the fence.[37] The fence or the hedge was the symbolic boundary between civilisation (the village) and the wilderness (the for-

<hr />

37 Duerr, H. *Dreamtime: Concerning the Boundary Between Wilderness and Civilisation*, p. 46.

est that lies beyond it). This state of wilderness was the home of the demonic Other (witches, faeries and nature spirits) who were a threat to the civilised world. On an esoteric level the hedge represents the non-physical, psychic boundary between the material world and the spirit world. The 'hedge rider' or 'hedge witch' is a special person who has the ability to cross over from side to the Other.

The distaff is a feminine tool and it is a cleft stick that holds wool or flax used in spinning and weaving. Symbolically it refers to the 'distaff side' or female descent through the mother. Because it is used in spinning and weaving, in pagan times it was a symbol of the goddess or goddesses controlling fate and destiny, death and the underworld. Finally, fennel is a magical plant associated with strength, virile power, fertility and also psychic protection.

Once the witches had reached the meeting ground where the Sabbath was to be held, travelling either physically or by spirit travel, they made obeisance to the presiding Devil, who was probably the chief male witch, dressed in a horned mask and animal costume. Sometimes the Devil read out a roster of those present from a 'black book'. A fire was then lit and the Horned One sat on a throne to receive the worship of his followers. At his side was a woman who was the leading female witch, known as the 'Queen of the Sabbath'. The witches saluted the Devil by means of the *osculum infame* or 'obscene kiss', which was given 'under the tail'. It has been suggested this practice was a debased form of a magical practice inherited by the European witch cult from the Saracen mystery schools. Certain parts of the initiate's body were breathed on by the Saracen adepts to activate the psychic centres or chakras.[38] Alternatively, the assembled witches bow to the Devil, bend their knees in supplication and "kick their legs high up so that their heads are bent back and their chins point to the sky" and "They turn their backs and, going backwards like crabs, put out their hands to touch him in supplication."[39]

In English and Scottish accounts of the Witches' Sabbath, it is at this point that the Devil or witch master instructed his adherents in various forms of magical practice, usually of a malefic type such as using poppets or wax images to cause harm. In the Continental accounts it was claimed that the proceedings usually continued with various acts of anti-Christian sacrilege or blasphemy such as spitting or trampling on the cross, defiling the host, the sacrifice of new-born babies to the Horned One and anything else the twisted minds of the Inquisitors could invent.

The feast was next on the agenda and again the witch-hunters made sure that the descriptions given under torture of the food eaten was suitably unpalatable such as rancid water, stale bread or unsalted meat (sometimes the flesh of unbaptised children). In reality, the witches seem to have provided their own food, although sometimes this was done by the 'Devil.' In the trial of the Pendle witches in Lancashire in 1612 a defendant called Old Chattox told the court that at the witch meets she attended:

38 Liddell, E. W. *The Pickingill Papers*, pp. 78–80.
39 Guazzo in his *Compendium Maleficarum* (1626).

Basque Witches, by Martin Van Maele, from Michelet's
La Sorciere.

"There were victuals, viz. flesh, butter, cheese, bread and drink." The North Berwick coven in 16th century Scotland followed their feast with whiskey and beer that had been home-made.

After the feast had ended, the social aspect of the meeting began. This included dancing in a circle or a ring or 'back to back' with music provided by one or more of the male witches playing on a flute, fiddle, drum, Jew's harp or sometimes the bagpipes. At the trial of the Scottish witch Isobel Gowdie in the 17th century it was said that the Devil would whip anyone who was slow at dancing or lagged behind, hence the popular term "May the Devil take the hindmost." From the descriptions of the dancing at the Sabbath there are indications that the witches may have fallen into a trance-like state akin to that experienced through the spirit flight. In his *Antidote to Atheism* written in 1653, Henry More quoted a boy who had attended a Sabbath and sat in a tree piping as the witches danced below. Seeing the wild movements, they were making, he exclaimed: "Good God, what a mad company have we here" Magical passes, postures, and music/dances are often inducers of trance or out-of-body experience, as with voudon, and serve as a preliminaries for spirit possession.

According to the Inquisition, the Witches' Sabbath ended with a sexual orgy that involved every imaginable perversion including bestiality and incest. The witches also allegedly had sexual relations with *incubi* and *succubi* spirits that were supposed to be present at the rite and with the Devil himself. The witch-hunters made a point of claiming that intercourse with Satan was always painful and unpleasant because of the abnormal size of his penis and the fact that his semen was icy cold. It is probable that the sexually repressed Inquisitioners exaggerated the orgiastic aspects of the Sabbath. However, the modern occultist Kenneth Grant has described the ritual as "a form of mass hysteria which releases almost unlimited quantities of pre-conceptual and atavistic energy'."

Grant claims the Witches' Sabbath was celebrated by "a priest-magician who assumed a particular god form [i.e., the Devil]". The witches used the Sabbatic rituals as a focus to produce a form of ecstasy during each of them 'assumed the god form' or, in magical terminology, became as a god. At this time each of the celebrants became divinely possessed and would have been endowed with superhuman powers. In such a state the witches could either bring into manifestation their own secret desires, wishes and fantasies or the psychic energy raised by the sex rites could be used for communal ends.[40]

It has been suggested that the spirit flight using the besom or broomstick may have had erotic or sexual connotations. There are references to the broomsticks used by witches as being carved at one end with a representation of the phallus concealed in the brush. Sometimes this was used in fertility rites to obtain a good harvest, but it may have also been employed to facilitate spirit flight to the Sabbath. In 1617 Margaret Ine Quane and her son were burnt alive in the market square of Castletown on the Isle of Man for practicing witchcraft. It was

40 Grant, K. *Aleister Crowley and the Hidden God*, p. 134.

claimed that she was in possession of a phallic-headed besom on which she 'rode' through the fields to bring a good harvest. An illustration of the execution of this Manx witch and her son was published in Gerald Gardner's book *The Meaning of Witchcraft*.[41]

The user of the riding stick or pole for fertility purposes as described in the Isle of Man example features in the modern Sabbatic Craft and provides a link between it and historical accounts of the spirit flight to the Witches' Sabbath. Andrew D. Chumbley of the Cultus Sabbati has written about a ritual inherited from one of his Old Craft initiators known as *To Go Forth by Night* and he specifically links it with the "night-flying hag upon the besom" and the Wild Hunt. Chumbley says that in the present-day Essex Craft initiates undertake solitary practices that combine dream-control with 'going forth by night' to the Sabbath.[42]

Knowledge of this nocturnal rite as passed down to Chumbley was based on the practice of a rural circle of wise-women in Buckinghamshire encountered by one of his initiators in the late 1940s, although evidently they and the ritual date back further than that period, and possibly to the 1880s. It was practised at Lammastide in early August or as soon as the first field had been harvested. The witches 'rode' on either a horse-headed rod or a forked stave through the yet-uncut sheaves and the stubble left from earlier cutting. This was known as "going forth

41 Aquarian Press, 1959.
42 Chumbley, Andrew D. "Cultus Sabbati: Dream, Provenance and Magistry" and 'A Scattering of Dust From the Wings of a Moth" in *Opuscula Magica* Vol. 2, pp. 65 and 67.

by night among the fields, riding through thick and thin in order to make the land fertile." The steps of the 'ride' were "danced into the land" to dispel or appease the old powers of decay and usher in the powers of increase. Chumbley compares this ritual dance with the actions of the Italian *benandanti*, magicians described by Dr Carlos Ginzburg who also 'go forth by night' to counter threats to the gathering in of the harvest and to aid the benevolent powers of nature.[43]

The ritualistic role of the horse-headed rod, as inherited by the Cultus Sabbati from its founding Old Craft lineages and featured in the modern Sabbatic Craft, is as the fetishistic symbol of the magical 'steed' that carries the witch on her spirit flight to the Sabbath and the Otherworld. It is equivalent in its nature and use to the traditional witches' besom and the spirit animals they used as mounts. As such it is a fetish object that represents both the steed ridden by a mortal and mortals actually as the steeds of the Old Gods. In this sense the 'rider' and the 'horse' are one entity.

An alternative use of the horse-headed rod in Sabbatic Craft is as a stick to beat the drum in the circle-dance. This facilitated a trance state where the 'fetch' or spirit of the witch, sometimes in animal form, left her body. This allowed her to "ride forth among the living and the dead" in the cavalcade of the Wild Hunt and experience the Witches' Sabbath as the Otherworldly assembly of spirits, therianthropic entities and faeries. A knotted cord or hair

43 Ibid., p. 68.

from the tail of a horse attached to the rod also creates a scourge, which stimulates the dancers in the circle to achieve a climax of frenzy and (sometimes sexual) ecstasy.[44] As previously mentioned, there are accounts in the witch trials of the covine leader beating 'the hindmost'—those who lagged behind in the Sabbath dance.

Some writers have claimed that, because the wearing of underwear was not that common in medieval Europe, when the witch sat astride the broomstick it came into direct contact with her perineum, the area of skin between the vagina and the anus. It is alleged that this is how the 'flying ointment' rubbed on the handle of the besom entered her bloodstream. James Endredy has described his experiences with a modern form of indigenous witchcraft in Mexico whose practitioners use 'dream trance'. This involves taking the Devil's Weed or the datura plant to release the spirit from the body (astral projection) so it can 'fly' to the spirit world. He describes watching a witch prepare a special potion from the plant and introduce it into her body by placing the end of a broomstick in her vagina. She explained that it was safer to do this to facilitate 'flying' than actually ingesting the potion into her stomach.[45]

An interesting early account of the Witches' Sabbath as practiced by people who the Inquisition regarded as Christian heretics rather than witches per se, provides evidence for its practice on both a mate-

44 Chumbley, *Azoëtia*, p. 104.
45 Endredy, J. *The Flying Witches of Vera Cruz*, pp. 88–89.

rial and spiritual level that connects with the erotic use of the broomstick. In 1477 Antionette Rose of Villars-Chabod in Savoy was examined by the Inquisition because she was believed to be a heretic. She said that at a time when she was short of money to redeem her land a local man called Mosset Gratin offered her a way out of her financial predicament. One evening he took her to a place nearby where there were a large group of men and women dancing and feasting. There she met the Devil, who was called Robinet and appeared "in the guise of a black man". Rose was told by Gratin to renounce God, the Catholic faith and "the whore called the Virgin Mary." Instead she was told she should accept Robinet as her lord and master and in return she would be given gold and silver. She then paid homage to the Devil by kissing him on the foot and in return he marked her on the little finger.

After treading on the cross with her left foot and breaking it "so as to spite God", Rose gave the Horned One her soul in exchange for the promised riches. Then the Devil gave her a wand about eighteen inches long and a box of ointment. She was told that if she rubbed the wand with the ointment, placed it between her thighs and said: "Go by the Devil, go!" she would be carried through the air to the place where the 'synagogue' or Sabbath was being held. The anomalous components in this relation of the Sabbath are curious, as is the suggestion of narcotic induction of flight applied through an eroto-magical technique.

In Sicily, historical witches were known as the 'Ladies from Outside', because they were often confused with faeries. Between 1579 and 1651 the Inquisitional tribunal at Palermo examined sixty-five cases of alleged witchcraft involving men and women travelling to witch meets held by faery 'companies' where the Good Folk and humans allegedly gathered together. These were presided over by a female divinity or her human representative known variously as the 'Queen of the Fairies', 'The Matron', 'The Fate', 'the Greek Lady' or the 'Wise Sybil'. She appeared as a beautiful young woman dressed in either black or white, but with cloven hooves instead of feet and cat's paws instead of hands.

In 1588 a fisherman's wife from Palermo described how she was transported through the air with her 'companie' of fellow witches riding on goats to a plain near Naples in Italy. There a man and a woman sat on thrones and were addressed as the 'king and queen'. She was made to swear on a book 'with large letters' that she would renounce the Christian God and the Virgin Mary. Instead she would worship them with her body and soul and in return they would give her beauty, wealth and many young lovers. The woman confessed that all this "seemed to be taking place in a dream." However, while she always slept naked, when she was the Witches' Sabbath she was fully clothed. At other witch meetings she had attended, the woman claimed that the participants shapeshifted into animal form. Also it appeared that the female leader who presided over the gatherings was sometimes chosen from among the human attendants. A fortune-teller confessed she had been made the 'queen of the witches' and all the other woman had to bow their heads in obedience to her.

She had done the same when another female witch was elected as the 'queen' for the night.[46]

In Eastern European accounts of witch meetings the participants told of being physically taken from their beds at night and transported to another place, sometimes a fairytale type castle in a dense forest where they danced with the faeries. In describing these experiences Dr Eva Pócs has said that in early modern Hungarian witchcraft, for instance, the popular Witches' Sabbath, uninfluenced by demonology, was generally a gathering of the witches, their spirit doubles and their bewitched victims, and it took place in an alternative world. She goes on to say that the Sabbaths were primarily connective events between the two worlds (the material and spiritual).[47] In these Hungarian accounts the event usually took place, whether on a material or spiritual level, on a mound, hill or mountaintop. Dr Pócs claims this is because in ancient mythology these locations were symbolic of the universal centre of the world.[48] Such physical features in the landscape are also traditionally associated with the Faerie realm. Dr Pócs states quite categorically that the worlds of faeries and witches were connected in the evidence given at the witch trials. She adds that these links only became polarised when witchcraft was demonised by the Church.[49] The modern demonologist and Roman Catholic writer on witchcraft

---

46 Henningsen, G. 'The Ladies From Outside' in *Early Modern Witchcraft*, p. 197. 47. Pócs, E. *Between the Living and the Dead*, pp. 73–74.

47 Pócs, E. *Between the Living and the Dead*, pp. 73–74.

48 Ibid., p. 90.

49 Ibid., pp 90–91.

Montague Summers said that the Witches' Sabbath
was

> *generally held in wooded spots, or on moun-*
> *tains and in caves. Such areas radiate between*
> *the world of men and the kingdom of Hell, so*
> *that Satan—sometimes a costumed degener-*
> *ate, other times an actual shade—might join*
> *the celebrants.*[50]

Although Summers was writing from a traditional
Christian perspective his comments reflect the ancient belief in the juxtaposition of the spirit world
with Middle Earth or the material plane.

In 1662 Isobel Gowdie, the Scotswoman accused of witchcraft, freely confessed that she had
travelled by spirit flight to a mound where she met
the faery king and queen. She added that she had
been frightened by the 'elf bulls' that guarded the
entrance to the Hollow Hill, an anomalous compo-
nent of spirit- flight suggesting she was describing
a real experience or at least one that was all too real
to her.[51] Central European accounts also mention
witches who travelled to the Venusburg mountain.
There they met with 'Dame Venus', the queen of the
faeries, and she taught them herbal knowledge and
healing techniques.

As we have previously seen in the account of the
so-called 'phantoms of the night' in the Alpine region, spirit travel to witch meetings was often as-

---

50 Summers, Montague. *The History of Witchcraft and Demonology*.
51 Seth, R. *In the Name of the Devil*, p. 106.

Brocken scene, artist unknown.

sociated with the shades of the dead. In popular
folk belief the spirit journey to Witches' Sabbath
was closely linked to the pan-European legend of
the Wild Hunt or Furious Horde that rode the night
sky. This was led by either a male or female semi-
divine, divine or heroic figure such as Woden, Diana,
Dame Holda, Harlequin, Herodias, King Arthur or
Cain and in later times the Devil. The company of
the Hunt consisted of a pack of devil-dogs or hell-
hounds accompanied by the spirits of unbaptised
children, the souls of the damned who had led wick-
ed lives and demons (often taking the pagan form of
woodwoses, 'wild women' and nature spirits). The
leader of the Hunt acted as a psychopomp or guide
to the dead on their way to the underworld and its
purpose was to gather up the spirits of the newly-
departed.

The ecstatic trances of the witches that led to
spirit flight gave them access to the dual worlds of
'the living and the dead'. This was recognised by
the alchemist Paracelsus (1493–1541) who merged
the concept of the 'Furious Army' or Wild Hunt
with the flight of the witches to the Sabbath. His
reasoning was based on the fact that both witches
and the Hunt were supposed to fly through the air
at night and both owed their allegiance to the powers of darkness. Both the shades of the dead and the
spirit-travelling witches seemed to have followed set
routes across the landscape. In the case of the company or 'procession' of the dead, in the Upper Valais
they were said to wander past nine mountains and
ninety-nine cemeteries along specific paths. These

were called 'people's paths', 'noisy paths' or 'processional paths'.[52]

Folklorist Bob Dickenson has found references in Lincolnshire to 'hedge riding' witches who travelled along so-called 'witch ways' or 'hex ways' across the countryside, either in human form or shapeshifted into hares. Information on this practice is found in *The Witches' Death Song*, whose twenty verses were sung by an old Lincolnshire wise woman on her deathbed. One verse refers to 'the Lord' taking the witches "over dykes and fields, straight away to Heaven." Dickenson believes this is a reference to the use of 'spirit paths' by the witches to travel to the Sabbath.[53]

Recent research into ley lines or landscape straight alignments has revealed new information and insights into the idea of night flying witches. Paul Devereaux, a former editor of *The Ley Hunter* magazine, believes that the leys that cross open countryside linking ancient sites were originally associated with actual prehistoric roads or trackways, the marking out of tribal boundaries, the cult of sacred kingship and travel to the spirit world. He has pointed out that in many ancient shamanic beliefs, spirits are said to travel in straight lines. In pagan times shrines were sited on these landscape alignments, usually at crossroads, in honour of wayside gods such as Hermes, Woden and Hecate. Crossroads are traditionally the site of gatherings of witches and are also associated with the Wild Hunt.

---

52 Behringer, W. *Shaman of Oberstdorf*, p. 33.
53 Ibid., pp. 6–15.

Devereaux and other researchers have found historical and folkloric references to so-called 'death roads', 'ghost paths', 'corpse ways' and 'faery paths'. These are always in a straight line and end in graveyards, at burial mounds and other ancient sites of religious importance. In medieval times corpses were carried along these special routes, even when they differed from normal roads that offered a quicker and easier passage. In folklore the faeries are often linked with the spirits of the dead and in Ireland, for instance, the Good Folk are regarded as the souls of the departed. The Scottish witch Bessie Dunlop confessed to having a spirit guide who had died in a battle some years before and he introduced her to the king and queen of the faeries who were accompanied by 'good women' or witches. It is still considered unlucky in parts of Ireland to build a house or a road that interferes with a known 'faery path'.

Paul Devereaux believes that these spirit paths were followed by night-flying witches and originally date back to Neolithic times. He claims that they acted as spiritual lines of communication between the physical and spirit worlds. There are many references in folk tradition, mythology and magical beliefs to the use of webs or threads for spirit travel. Such beliefs may be connected to the concept of ley lines, the 'web of wyrd' and also to the witch goddess as the weaver of fate or destiny.[54]

In ancient times the shaman contacted or accessed the Otherworld through an ecstatic trance during which his or her spirit body left its physical

54 Devereaux, P. *The Haunted Land*, pp. 119–122. 55. Ibid.

vessel. The techniques used to achieve this included ritual drumming, breathing exercises and the ingestion of naturally hallucinogenic plants. This spirit journey or spirit flight was translated into an actual journey along the spirit lines in the enchanted landscape. Eventually, in the post-Christian era, these spiritual alignments became identified with material routes and landmarks in the physical landscape. These were ancient trackways, the so-called 'death roads' or 'royal roads', and ancient sacred sites such as stone circles, standing stones and burial mounds. In Paul Devereux's opinion, the spirit lines are connected to gateways leading to other levels of reality and these can be accessed during altered states of consciousness. Such experiences he believes gave rise to the folkloric stories of witches flying on broomsticks to the Sabbath, human visits to the realm of Faerie and the Wild Hunt riding the midwinter sky.[55]

Dr Éva Pócs also speaks of the 'levels and crossings' used by Eastern European witches to pass from one world to another, stating that "the alternative world that appeared in visions or dreams was part of 'normal' existence and that there was a path between the two. The smooth continuity of events and the web of cause and effect interwove between the two worlds, and the motion of both, were seen as the same reality". She goes on to say that the supernatural and the Otherworld were physical realities and a part of everyday life for those who perceived them. In fact, it was just as likely or possible for a

55 Ibid.

person to enter the Otherworld using their spirit double as it was for the dead to enter the physical world.[56]

Writing in *The Ley Hunter* magazine, Nigel Aldcroft Jackson has pointed out that the Wild Hunt is often associated with specific locations in the countryside and routes across it. He quoted a 19th century source who said:

> *There are often places where Woden is accustomed to feed his horse or let it graze, and in those places the wind is always blowing. He has a preference for certain tracks and which he hunts again and again at fixed seasons, from which circumstances certain districts and villages in the Saxon land received the name of Woden's Way.*

Jackson notes that on Dartmoor the 'Hell Hounds' are said to hunt the souls of the dead along the Abbot's Way, an ancient trackway that dates back to prehistoric times.[57]

In modern times the principles of Sabbatic Witchcraft have been expressed through the writings of the late Andrew D. Chumbley and other initiates of Cultus Sabbati, such as Daniel A. Schulke and Robert Fitzgerald. However one recent exponent of the Sabbatic mysteries was an influence on Chumbley's writing and artwork: the psychic artist, occultist,

---

56 Pócs, E. *Between the Living and the Dead*, p. 93.
57 Jackson, N. 'Trance, Ecstasy and the Furious Host'. *The Ley Hunter* #117, p. 8.

magician and visionary medium Austin Osman Spare (1886–1956).

Spare was born in Holborn, London and was the son of a policeman. He began to draw as a young boy and when he was thirteen his parents enrolled him for evening classes at Lambeth Art School in South London. After working for a poster design company and a stained glass manufacturer, Spare took a scholarship at the Royal College of Art. He has been described by his friend and fellow occultist, Kenneth Grant, as "one of the most accomplished graphic artists of his day."[58] Despite having several private exhibitions of his artwork praised by the critics, various circumstances led Spare to turn his back on the art establishment. He was to end his life living in poverty in the slums of South London eking out a meagre living by drawing portraits of local characters in nearby public houses and selling talismans and amulets to fellow occult practitioners.

However, what concerns us here is not the minutiae of Austin Spare's life, but his occult work and connection with traditional witchcraft. Although he was a member of Aleister Crowley's magical group the A.A. or Argentium Astrum (the Brotherhood of the Silver Star), he and the Great Beast 666 did not always agree on matters magical. Crowley in fact condemned Spare as a 'black magician', although paradoxically he also held his disciple's occult insights in high esteem.[59]

---

58 Grant, K. *Images and Oracles of Austin Osman Spare*, p. 7.
59 Ibid., p. 8.

Copper engraving by J. Aliame after David Teniers'
drawing 'Arrival at the Sabbat'.

Spare in fact drew his esoteric inspiration from traditional witchcraft and Spiritualism. This was not such an unlikely pairing as in the 19th century some practitioners of the Craft hid their lights under the convenient cover of the new Spiritualist movement. Spare was, and still is, highly regarded by contemporary Spiritualists and, writing in the *Daily Express* newspaper in 1927, the Fleet Street journalist and leading Spiritualist Hannan Swaffer described him as 'a remarkable artist' and compared him to Gustav Dore and Aubrey Beardsley. Spare told Swaffer that much of his artwork was 'automatic drawing' and was executed either in a trance state or "while in a sort of dream." He added that the life of a hermit living in poverty had created the conditions for his psychic development.

Spare's early introduction to witchcraft came through meeting an elderly fortune-teller called Mrs Ruth Paterson. She made claims that she was connected with the famous Salem witches in America and through them with Native American spiritual traditions. Kenneth Grant believed her claim and has said that Spare's spirit guide, known as Black Eagle, was "a focus for the ancient Amerindian sorcery that once informed the witch cult in Salem, Mass., from which Mrs Paterson had drawn her magical power."[60] In later years Black Eagle manifested through Spare and helped him to produce automatic drawings that "emanate an atmosphere of ancient and broody evil."[61]

60 Ibid., p. 15.
61 Ibid.

Mrs Paterson, according to Spare, did have some remarkable powers including the ability to conjure up thought forms for her clients that were so vivid that they could physically materialise in the dark corners of her room. The old witch taught this technique to Spare and he demonstrated it once to two visitors who challenged him to summon up an elemental. Spare warned them against such an operation, but they insisted. He drew a magical sigil on a piece of white card, held it to his forehead and muttered a spell under his breath. A miasmic green mist began to appear in his basement flat and it formed itself into a shadowy mass with burning black eyes. It is said that one of the witnesses died shortly afterwards and the other lost his mind.[62] A startling painting by Spare of this elemental spirit features on the cover of the first edition of the 1970s weekly partwork magazine *Man, Myth and Magic*.

As well as conjuring spirits, Mrs Paterson also had the power to 'cast a glamour' over herself. When she did this the old crone was transformed into a beautiful young woman. This magical operation was closely linked with the modus operandi of the spirit flight to the Witches' Sabbath. Spare tells of boarding a bus in London one wet evening. The rain was heavy and persistent and as a result the streets were deserted as people sought shelter in shop doorways. Although the lower deck of the bus was empty, Spare went upstairs where, in those days, smokers could still practise their vice. He found a seat and gazed out of the window at the rainswept world out-

62 Ibid., p. 22.

side, which suddenly seemed strangely unfamiliar and unreal. He looked around at his fellow passengers, who oddly were all old women. They also appeared unreal to him and outside the normal range of awareness. When he left the bus, Spare offered his fare to the conductor and the man said he had not come upstairs to collect it as it was not worth the trip for only one passenger.

Spare speculated he had witnessed a company of witches in spirit form travelling to the Witches' Sabbath on a modern form of transport. This was confirmed to him by the fact that the women had made 'certain mysterious gestures', which had reminded him of those made by Mrs Paterson before her transformations from an old woman to a young one. He sensed that the women on the bus were on their way to the Sabbath and were in the process of a similar transformation.[63] Spare's own experiences with his 'witch-mother' had convinced him of the reality of the Sabbath as a method for establishing contact with elementals and familiar spirits capable of providing the witch or sorcerer with superhuman power and occult knowledge. Many of Spare's drawings and paintings depicted scenes from the Witches' Sabbath, and he used pen, pencil, crayon and paintbrush to illustrate the grotesque characters and elemental denizens of the Otherworld who attended these revels.

Kenneth Grant claims that the Witches' Sabbath experienced by Austin Spare under the tutelage of his witch teacher originated from 'ancient sources'

63 Ibid., pp. 23–24.

and "the mode of transvection which enabled the witch to attend the Sabbath was an astral phenomenon, and the unguent rubbed into the body was undoubtedly composed of sleep and ecstasy-producing ingredients." He adds that it is the nature of the astral plane to endow the Sabbatic rite "with the glamour of reality." [64] Spare's own view of the ritual was that it was based on the use of sex as a medium for a magical act to generate power. When this was released it could be used by the coven and "directed towards the furtherment of mass desire." The sexual act in a magical context was not a matter of personal satisfaction. Instead the adept controls, transmutes and directs the psychic energy it raises for an end purpose or desired result. In Spare's view, the purpose for celebrating the Witches' Sabbath, either on a physical or astral (psychic) level, was to perform a magical operation that created "the materialisation of wishful thinking". In fact, the purpose of sex magic is to concentrate on a desired result at the moment of orgasm, when psychic and physical energy is released, so it that can be used by the magician.

As a visionary artist, inspired writer and evocative poet Andrew D. Chumbley followed closely in the footsteps of Austin Osman Spare. In his *Azoëtia: A Grimoire of the Sabbatic Craft*, Chumbley wrote about the attendance at the Witches' Sabbath in terms that would have been easily understood by Spare. In the case of both these magical practitioners, their understanding of the arcane Sabbatic Mysteries was

64 Grant, K. *Aleister Crowley and the Hidden God,* p. 134.

based on the inheritance of secret wisdom from genuine Old Craft sources. Chumbley wrote of the use of the horse-headed rod that is "the steed that beareth the Spirit of the Adept unto the Sabbat" and as we have seen he compared it to the traditional witch's besom or broomstick. He also talked of the 'Body of Light' ascending as the "Body of Corporeal Substance descendeth into Sleep amid the Dead" and attracting "all manner of Ancestral Shades and Spirits."[65] In this respect the 'Body of Light' is the fetch or spirit double spoken of in folklore and witch tradition. It leaves the physical shell and travels to meet with the Good Companie at the crossroads of the Witches' Sabbath.

This then is the 'secret of secrets' within the Sabbatic Craft inherited and practised by its modern followers, encompassing the hidden tradition of spirit flight by moonlight to the Witches' Sabbath in the world of dreaming. While many speak of the 'Sabbatic Craft', we can see from this brief exposition of its belief and praxis that in reality it is specific to a particular form of traditional witchcraft. Its spiritual and psychic origins deeply rooted in a past both distant and ancient yet, in its continuing practice by dedicated followers of the Elder Faith and the Nameless Way, it still exists in our modern times as a living tradition. It is ageless and as such it is also eternal. Whenever the call to the Sabbath comes there will always be those who will mount their magical steeds to travel in the Dreamtime and attend the ancestral conclave of spirits, faeries and

65 *Azoëtia*, p. 56

humans. The Body of Light as reorientated in the Sabbatic Tradition is a beacon which generates the spirit retinue of Witchdom itself.

Witches' Sabbath, *Das Kloster*, 1845.

Bibliography

Andrews, George. *Drugs and Magic*. Panther Books: UK, 1975.

Ansell, Robert. *Borough Satyr: The Life and Art of Austin Osman Spare*. Fulgur Limited, UK 2005.

Behringer, Wolfgang. *Shaman of Oberstdorf*. University Press of Virginia, 1998.

Beskin, Geraldine and Boner, John (ed). *Austin Osman Spare: Artist Occultist Sensualist*. The Beskin Press, UK 1999.

Briggs, Robin 'Dangerous Spirits: Shapeshifting, Apparitions, and Fantasy in Lorraine Witchcraft Trials' in *Werewolves, Witches and Wandering Spirits*. Kathryn A. Edwards (ed). Truman State University Press, 2002.

Byrne, Patrick. *Witchcraft in Ireland*. The Mercer Press, Ireland 1967.

Campbell, Joseph. *The Portable Jung.* Penguin Books, UK 1985.

Carrington, Dorothy. *The Dream Hunters of Corsica.* Weidenfeld & Nicolson, UK 1995.

Chumbley, Andrew D. *Azoëtia: A Grimoire of the Sabbatic Craft.* Xoanon, UK 1992; Sethos Edition, USA 2002.

————— . "The Golden Chain and the Lonely Road" in *Opuscula Magica: Volume 1; Essays on Witchcraft and the Sabbatic Tradition.* Three Hands Press, USA 2010.

————— . 'Cultus Sabbati: Dream, Provenance and Magistry' and 'A Scattering of Dust From the Wings of a Moth' in *Opuscula Magica: Volume 2: Essays on Witchcraft and Crooked Path Sorcery.* Three Hands Press, 2011.

Devereaux, Paul. *The Haunted Land.* Piatkus, UK 2001. Dickenson, Bob. 'Lincolnshire Spirit Lines' in *Markstone* # 8 UK, Spring, 1993.

Duerr, Hans Peter. Dreamtime: *Concerning the Boundary Between Wilderness and Civilization.* Basil Blackwell, UK 1985.

Durring, Jack. 'I Attended a Witches' Sabbath'. *Fate* USA 1963.

Endredy, James. *The Flying Witches of Vera Cruz.* Llewellyn, USA 2011.

Ginzburg, Dr Carlos. *The Night Battles.* Routledge & Kegan Paul, UK 1983.

——— . *Ecstasies: Deciphering the Witches' Sabbath.* Hutchinson Radius, UK 1990.

——— . 'Deciphering the Witches' Sabbath' in *Early Modern European Witchcraft*, G. Henningson, G and Ankarloo, B. Clarendon Press, UK 1993.

Grant, Kenneth. *Aleister Crowley and the Hidden God.* Frederick Muller Ltd., UK 1973.

——— . *Cults of the Shadow.* Frederick Muller Ltd., UK 1975.

——— . *Images and Oracles of Austin Osman Spare.* Fulgur Limited, UK 2003.

Hansen, Harold A. *The Witch's Garden.* Unity Press, Santa Cruz 1978.

Henningsen, Gustav 'The Ladies From Outside' in *Early Modern Witchcraft*, G. Henningsen, G and Ankarloo, B. eds. Clarendon Press, UK 1993.

Howard, Michael. 'Flying Witches: The *Unguenti Sabbati* in Traditional Witchcraft' in *Witchcraft and Shamanism,* Clifton, Professor Chas. S. ed. Llewellyn USA, 1994.

Jackson, Nigel 'Trance, Ecstasy and the Furious Host' in *The Ley Hunter* #117, UK 1992.

Jung, Carl. *Memories, Dreams, Reflections.* Vintage House, USA 1985.

King, Francis. *Ritual Magic in England.* Neville Spearman, 1970.

Kuklin, Alexander. *How Do Witches Fly?* AceN Press, USA 1999.

Lecouteux, Professor Claude. *Witches, Werewolves and Fairies.* Inner Traditions, USA 2003.

Liddell, E. W. *The Pickingill Papers.* Capall Bann, UK 1994.

Peuckert, Will-Erich. "Hexensalben" in *Medizinischer Monatsspiegel*, 8th part, August 1960, Darmstadt 1960.

Pócs, Dr Éva. *Fairies and Witches in SE and Central Europe.* Svonaltanen Tiedakanatan, Finland 1983.

————. *Between the Living and the Dead.* Central European University Press, Hungary 1999.

Robbins, Russell Hope. *Encyclopedia of Witchcraft and Demonology.* Hamlyn Publishing Company, UK 1959.

Rogers, Thomas. *The Midwife and the Witch.* Yale University Press, 1966.

Ronay-Dougal, Dr Serena. *Where Science and Magic Meet.* Element, UK 1991.

Rycroft, Charles. *The Innocence of Dreams.* Oxford University Press, UK 1981.

Schulke, Daniel A. *Veneficium: Magic, Witchcraft and the Poison Path.* Three Hands Press, USA 2012.

Scot, *Reginald Discoverie of Witchcraft.* 1584, Centaur Press, UK edition 1964.

Seth, Ronald. *In the Name of the Devil.* Jarrold, UK 1969.

Simmons, Marc. *Witchcraft in the Southwest: Spanish and Indian Supernaturalism* on the

Rio Grande. Bison Books, USA 1974.

Summers, Montague. *The History of Witchcraft and Demonology.* Rider, UK 1956.

Teller, Joanne and Blackwater, Norman. *The Navaho Skinwalker, Witchcraft and Related Phenomena.* Infinity Horn Publishers, USA 1997.

Watkins, Mary. *Walking Dreams.* Spring Publications, USA 1986.

By Moonlight and Spirit Flight was printed & bound at Midwinter, 2019 in an edition of two thousand two hundred twenty-two impressions. Of these are 1,700 softcover copies, 500 hand-numbered hardcover copies in brown cloth with colour dust jacket, and 22 hand-numbered deluxe copies in full umber Nigerian goat with slipcase. Fine bindings were executed by The Key Printing & Binding, Oakland, California.

SCRIBÆ QUO MYSTERIUM FAMULATUR